For 2/5/2000

Roberta
from Eileen

A Friend
for
All Seasons

Compiled by
Helen H. Moore

Illustrated by C. James Frazier

Book designed by Arlene Greco

PETER PAUPER PRESS, INC.
WHITE PLAINS, NEW YORK

*To Mary McMullen, Connie Giesa, and
Lydia Gorski, my first friends*

Make new friends, but keep the old.
One is silver, the other gold.

Original artwork copyright © 1998
C. James Frazier,
licensed by Wild Apple Licensing

Text copyright © 1998
Peter Pauper Press, Inc.
202 Mamaroneck Avenue
White Plains, NY 10601
All rights reserved
ISBN 0-88088-084-8
Printed in China
7 6 5 4 3 2

Contents

Introduction

What *is* a friend for all seasons?
To me, such a friend is a steadfast
companion on the journey
through all the seasons of one's
life. Friends for all seasons stick
together in all weather. Basking
together in the sunshine of life's
summers, sheltering one another
through life's winter storms, they
make the good times better and
the bad times less bad.

In this book you will find
thoughts about friendship from
the famous and the anonymous, in
forms ranging from folk wisdom
to philosophy, from wisecracks to

poetry. There are ideas about how to make a friend, the proper "functions" of friends, how to choose friends wisely, the inestimable value of a good friend, and more. The quotes come from all ages and all times, because, in all times in history and all places on earth, it has always been important to have "a friend for all seasons."

I hope the thoughts and feelings you will find in these pages will give you fuel to make the fires of your own friendships burn brighter, in all seasons.

H. H. M.

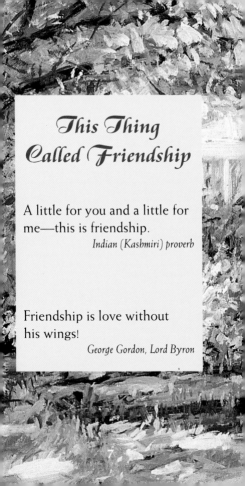

This Thing
Called Friendship

A little for you and a little for me—this is friendship.

Indian (Kashmiri) proverb

Friendship is love without his wings!

George Gordon, Lord Byron

A good friend is worth more
than a bad sister.
Serbo-Croatian proverb

Friendship improves happiness,
and abates misery, by doubling
our joy, and dividing our grief.
Joseph Addison

A true friend at your side is
better than gold on your finger.
Welsh proverb

Real friends will share: even a
strawberry!
Russian proverb

A friend loveth at all times . . .
Proverbs 17:17 (KJV)

Friendship is the inexpressible comfort of feeling safe with a person, having neither to weigh thoughts nor measure words.

George Eliot

Life has no blessing like a prudent friend.

Cicero

There is no better mirror than an old friend.

Japanese proverb

To meet an old friend in a distant land is like refreshing rain after a drought.

Chinese proverb

True friendship is like a single soul split into two bodies.

Mexican proverb

Love is only chatter,
Friends are all that matter.

Gelett Burgess,
Willy and the Lady

On Finding and Making Friends

I am treating you as my friend, asking you to share my present *minuses* in the hope I can ask you to share my future *pluses*.

Katherine Mansfield

Be a friend to yourself, and others will befriend you.

Scottish proverb

It always amazes me that in life
the most unexpected people
sometimes are the ones who
throw you the life preserver.

Ali MacGraw,
Moving Pictures

Make another person feel
welcome. Surprise them. Smile.

Tina Kelley

The friend that can be bought is
not worth buying.

Irish proverb

Remember that friends should be
built for endurance, not speed.

Patricia McGinn Moore

A home-made friend wears longer than one you buy in the market.

Austin O'Malley

Be slow to fall into friendship; but when thou art in, continue firm and constant.

Socrates

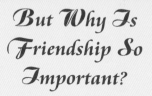

But Why Is Friendship So Important?

Friendships are a balm in the passages of life.

Clare Ansberry

It is better, given the choice, to have friends.

Elizabeth Bishop,
On her refusal to write criticism

Friends broaden your horizons, teach you how to find common ground with people who are different from you. Friends provide a network of support outside your immediate family. . . . You can tell friends your secrets, your fears, even your most awful jokes and you can ask them for advice. Friends can be loyal and reliable, sympathetic and caring.

Catherine O'Neill Grace

When friends meet, the heart is warm.

Scottish proverb

From the hand of a friend, a stone is an apple.

Arabic proverb

Where your friends are, there are your riches.

German proverb

They seem to take the sun out of the world that take friendship out of life.

Cicero

Friendship is one of the most tangible things in a world which offers fewer and fewer supports.

Kenneth Branagh

You should never say goodbye to a friend. Remember, friends are a lot harder to get than relatives.

Marilyn vos Savant

Each Friend
Is Different

Each friend represents a world
in us, a world possibly not born
until they arrive, and it is only
by this meeting that a new
world is born.

Anaïs Nin

A Friend is a poem.

Persian proverb

A friend is:
Someone who is able to
accept your need—no, your
right—to change and grow.

Someone who will do any-
thing for you, and ask nothing
in return.

Someone I can trust to see the
real me, inside and out.

Someone who will go on a
diet, just to keep you compa-
ny, even though she doesn't
need to lose weight.

Someone I can sit quietly
with, if that's how I feel.

Someone who, when you spot them walking down the street or in the supermarket parking lot, makes you break out in a smile.

Someone who can tell you you look fat in those pants, but in a nice way.

Someone who doesn't say "I told you so," even though she did, and she was right. She doesn't have to rub it in. She wouldn't even want to.

A friend is truly sorry when things are going bad for me, and truly happy when I have my little successes in life.

A friend will give you the last
chocolate graham cracker,
even though it's her favorite.

> (Answers to the question
> "What is a friend?" given by various
> women and girls, asked of teachers
> and students at a day-care center.)

A friend is someone who will
take the baby for a week.

> *Dorothy*, an overwrought new mother,
> quoted by Letty Cottin Pogrebin,
> Among Friends

Friends are like stars; and
sometimes, on a gentle summer
night or in the clear, cold, still-
ness of winter, it's enough to
look up at them, and admire the
way they shine.

Helen H. Moore

So That's What Friends Are For

We were sounding boards.
That's what friends are for.

Mary Wohleber

A faithful friend is the
medicine of life . . .

Ecclesiasticus 6:16

The best friendships, those that nourish the soul and spirit, survive and even thrive over time and distance.

Lydia A. Mayo

I am beginning to notice something about Pat Sonnier. In each of his letters he expresses gratitude and appreciation for my care. He makes no demands. He doesn't ask for money. He does not request my phone number. . . . He only says how glad he is to have someone to communicate with because he has been so lonely.

Sister Helen Prejean,
Dead Man Walking

Our parents could not under-
stand our thoughts, but our
friends could and thought they
were wonderful and were telling
us, "You said the funniest thing
last night." We deeply needed
that because our parents were
still saying, "Be sure to wear your
boots because it's raining out."

Joan Rivers

Your boss is mad; your spouse is
complaining; the kids are
cranky; and you just discovered
that the roof is leaking. There's
only one thing to do. Pick up
the phone and call a friend.

Lois Wyse

To a Friend

I love you
Because you have done
More than any creed
Could have done
To make me good,
And more than any fate
Could have done
To make me happy.
You have done it
Without a touch,
Without a word,
Without a sign.
You have done it
By being yourself,
Perhaps that is what
Being a friend means
After all.

Anonymous

You don't have to play games with a friend. You don't have to pretend you are someone you're not. A friend is a person you can count on . . . and who can count on you for emotional support.

Adelaide Bry

Who paces the hospital corridors during surgery? Who sleeps by the bedside on a cot, calls the distant relatives with news, asks doctors for the prognosis? Who fills the prescriptions, buys the groceries, bird-dogs the insurance claims? Who holds the power of attorney? Who shares memories of the past, plans for the future and musings about mortality? The answer, increasingly, is friends.

Jane Gross

Venus and Mars on Friendship

Children grow and go; even
beloved men sometimes seem to
be beaming their perceptions
and responses in from a different
planet. But our female friends
are forever.

Anna Quindlen

Platonic friendship: The interval
between the introduction and
the first kiss.

Sophie Irene Loeb

Men kick friendship around like a football, but it doesn't seem to crack. Women treat it like glass and it goes to pieces.

Anne Morrow Lindbergh

We may neglect friends when family or work consume our time and energy. We need friends less—or need fewer friends—at certain points in our lives. Or we may have the least energy for friends when we most need them. But women know that friendships matter deeply.

Harriet Lerner

We shelter children for a time;
we live side by side with men;
and that is all. We owe them
nothing, and are owed nothing.
I think we owe our friends more,
especially our female friends.

Fay Weldon

Women put their hands all over
each other and what is conveyed
is nothing more than what is
intended: feelings of genuine
fondness and communion.

Robin Abcarian

The thing needed . . . to raise
women (and to raise men, too)
is these friendships without love
between men and women. And
if between married men and
married women, all the better.

Florence Nightingale

I think women know how to be friends. That's what saves our lives.

Alice Adams

My true friends have always given me that supreme proof of devotion, a spontaneous aversion for the man I loved.

Colette

The truth is that friendship is to me every bit as sacred and eternal as marriage.

Katherine Mansfield

Nothing gives me more intense satisfaction than my friendship with Susan B. Anthony. Ours has been a friendship of hard work and self-denial. Emerson says "It is better to be a thorn in the side of your friend than his echo." If this adds weight and stability to friendship, then ours will endure forever, for we have indeed been thorns in the side of each other.

Elizabeth Cady Stanton

Friendship between women can take different forms. It can run like a river, quietly and sustainingly through life; it can be an intermittent, sometime thing; or it can explode like a meteor, altering the atmosphere so that nothing ever feels or looks the same again.

Molly Haskell

Love me, please; I love you. I can bear to be your friend. So ask of me anything . . .

Edna St. Vincent Millay

Then, Again . . .

In prosperity our friends know us; in adversity we know our friends.

John Churton Collins

What you give to a good friend is not lost.

Polish proverb

Friends may come, and friends
may go, but enemies accumulate.

Anonymous

Entertaining a valued friend of
embarrassing public habits is best
done in private. If she questions
why you prefer not to meet her
in public, you might gently say
that you do not wish to share
her attention with her many
admirers . . .

Judith Martin
(Miss Manners)

A friend you get for nothing: an
enemy has to be bought.

Yiddish proverb

The holy passion of friendship is of so sweet and steady and loyal and enduring a nature that it will last through a whole lifetime, if not asked to lend money.

Mark Twain

A friend is a person who stays by your side all through the troubles he's caused you.

Marilyn vos Savant

You should have contact with your closest friends through the most intimate and exclusive of all media—the telephone.

Andy Warhol

The Care and Maintenance of Friendships

Hold a true friend with both hands.

African (Kanuri) proverb

Good friends settle their accounts speedily.

Chinese proverb

If, instead of a jewel, or even a flower, one could cast the gift of a lovely thought into the heart of a friend, that would be giving as the angels must give.

Anonymous

Who wants to be adored? You want to be able to relate to a person, woman to woman.

Oprah Winfrey

One should go invited to a friend in good fortune, and uninvited in misfortune.

Swedish proverb

Do not remove a fly from your
friend's forehead with a hatchet.

Chinese proverb

Many a friend has been lost
through a joke, but none has
ever been gained so.

Czech proverb

If friends have faith in each
other, life and death are of no
consequence.

Chinese proverb

Be a listener. Listen, listen, listen. Don't judge what your hear, or change what you're hearing. They (friends) have to express certain things and your job is not to correct it. Let them say what they wish, even if you disagree or it hurts you.

Anne Rosberger,
Director, Bereavement and
Loss Center of New York

Friendship, like mud, breaks when it dries up.

Philippine proverb

Friendship is a pretty full-time occupation if you really are friendly with somebody. You can't have too many friends because then you're just not really friends.

Truman Capote

She who judges between two friends loses one of them.

French proverb

Correct your friends secretly and praise them publicly.

Italian proverb

The amount of good we can do with a glad heart and a smile is incalculable, and the good of it goes out to others and stays with us at the same time.

Dixie Carter

The friendship of two depends upon the forbearance of one.

Indian (Tamil) proverb

There is nothing so great that I fear to do it for my friend; nothing so small that I will disdain to do it for him.

Sir Philip Sidney

Do not keep the alabaster box of your love and tenderness sealed up until your friends are dead. Fill their lives with sweetness. Speak approving, cheering words while their ears can hear them, and while their hearts can be thrilled and made happier. The kind things you mean to say when they are gone, say before they go. The flowers you mean to send for their coffin, send to brighten and sweeten their homes before they leave them . . . Post-mortem kindness does not cheer the burdened heart; flowers on the coffin cast no fragrance backward over the weary way.

George W. Childs,
from essay, Friends

54

I have often thought that as longevity is generally desired, and I believe, generally expected, it would be wise to be continually adding to the number of our friends, that the loss of some may be supplied by others. Friendship, "the vine of life," should, like a well-stocked wine cellar, be thus continually renewed.

Samuel Johnson

"Give and take," good friendships make.

Scottish proverb

Finally, There Are Friends for All Seasons

I do not believe that friends are necessarily the people you like best, they are merely the people who got there first.

Peter Ustinov

Friends don't have to be the same age you are.

Catherine O'Neill Grace

Why was it that everybody
seemed to have more friends
when they were kids than when
they were adults?

Richard Price

Depth of friendship does
not depend upon length of
acquaintance.

Rabindranath Tagore

Accept your friends with all their
faults; after all, that's the way
you want them to accept you.

Portuguese proverb

They grow old together, savoring a shared past, unafraid of the future . . . They have experienced the same passages. They watched children grow, leave, and come back again, and parents, siblings, and spouses die. They grew up in the same era and value the same things . . .

Clare Ansberry

Old friends and old ways ought
not to be disdained.

Danish proverb

It is great to have friends when
one is young, but indeed it is still
more so when you are getting
old. When we are young, friends
are, like everything else, a matter
of course. In the old days we
know what it means to have
them.

Edvard Grieg

"Don't ask me to leave you. . . .
Wherever you go, I will go;
wherever you live, I will live.
Your people will be my people,
and your God will be my God.
Wherever you die, I will die, and
that is where I will be buried.
May the Lord's worst punish-
ment come upon me if I let anything but death separate me
from you!"

The Book of Ruth 1:16-17
(Good News Bible)

Old friends are the blessings of
long life.

Scottish proverb

I am wealthy in my friends.

William Shakespeare,
Timon of Athens

Life is to be fortified by many friendships. To love and to be loved is the greatest happiness of existence.

Sydney Smith

Friendship is the shadow of the evening, which strengthens with the setting sun of life.

Jean de La Fontaine

I want to be your friend
For ever and ever without break
    or decay.
When the hills are all flat
And the rivers are all dry,
When it lightens and thunders
    in winter,
When it rains and snows
    in summer,
When Heaven and Earth mingle
Not till then will I part from you.

Oaths of Friendship,
Chinese, 1st Century A.D.